CW00349104

# Hexham Remembered

*An illustrated glimpse into Hexham's past*

Compiled by
**Hilary Kristensen & Colin Dallison**

Wagtail Press

# Hexham Remembered

*Compiled by Hilary Kristensen & Colin Dallison*

*First Published March 2006*
*by Wagtail Press*
*Gairshield,*
*Steel, Hexham,*
*Northumberland*
*NE47 0HS*

*Designed by T. W. Kristensen*

*ISBN: 0-9538443-5-8*

*Cover illustrations:*
*Front - "Hexham Bridge End" by Ralph Hedley*
*Back - "Hexham Market Place" by William Bell Scott*

*Wagtail Press*

# Hexham Remembered

*This book gathers together old photographs, paintings and etchings which show both what has been lost and what still remains. Hexham today is a bustling market town with many buildings which reflect its historic past.*

HEXHAM ABBEY CHURCH.

## Contents

"*Hexham Market Place*" by William Bell Scott 1853

*plate 1*

# Market Place

*Right and Below*
This 1820 picture shows the window above the main entrance of the 17th century White Horse Inn. Known formerly as the Prior's House, the three shields to the right may be those of the Archbishop of York (fig.1).

*fig. 1*

The painting opposite shows Isabell, the landlady's daughter, sitting at the window above the entrance of the White Horse Inn.

*plate 2*

The artist William Bell Scott mentions his visit to the inn in his memoirs -
"I found myself in the old-fashioned, sleepy town of Hexham, and settled down in a small apartment in the half-timbered hostelry called the White Horse. This apartment was over the porch, and the front of it was one long narrow casement with a long bunker seat under it, looking out on the market-place and great church. This long window, with the casements opened and the market-place seen without, was my subject, and the landlady's daughter, posed to me at full length on the window seat knitting".

*plate 3*

The Allgood Pant (public fountain), near the west end of the Shambles, and the Moot Hall, 1830.

The White Horse Inn c.1856

This rare early photograph, showing the new roof, was taken just before the inn was demolished in February 1859 to make way for shops.

"January 26th 1771 - The ancient market cross, which formerly stood at Hexham, was removed down to Haydon Bridge"
*John Sykes       Historical Records.*

*plate 4*

plate 5

*Right*

The Shambles c.1830. This covered market was built in 1766 by Sir Walter Blackett, Lord of the Manor. It has stone columns on three sides and wooden columns on the sheltered south side. There was a butter, egg and poultry market on the south side and the back part was divided into butchers' stalls. The Shambles was repaired in 1877 by the Local Board of Health as a market and also as a place of public resort for the working men and artisans of the town.

> Tuesday is the weekly market-day, and there is an inferior market on Saturday. The markets are extremely well supplied. Meat is as good, as cheap, in as great plenty, as in any town. Poultry, eggs and butter, are cheap and in great plenty. Fish is scarce. The distance from the sea and the land carriage contract the supply and injure the quality, while they increase the price. Vegetables do not hold a high place in the market, from the number of gardens, which enables almost every family to raise its own stock.
>
> *History of Hexham 1823*

8

plate 6

*Right*

In the 1890s Mr W. Riddle married Miss Bell of Bell the chemist giving the shop a new name. Note the pestle & mortar above the shop name to represent the trade of the chemist.

*Below*

The Market Place c.1890, showing the shops built in 1859 to replace the old White Horse Inn. The large gas lamp was installed in 1884.

*plate 7*

*plate 8*   9

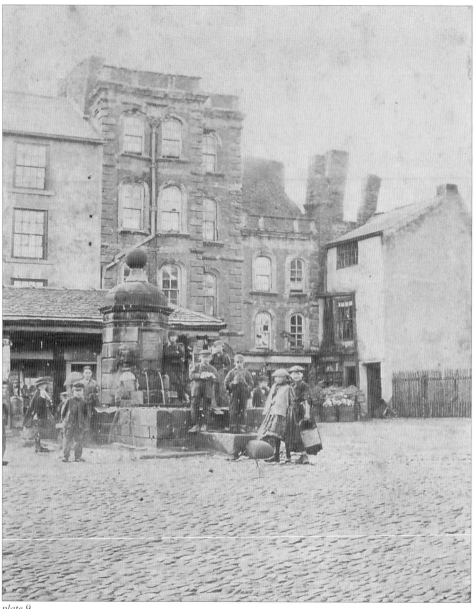

A rare early photograph showing the Allgood Pant which was removed in 1865 to allow free access to Beaumont Street. The public fountain had been presented to the town by Robert Allgood, Esq. The inscription read "Ex dono Roberti Allgood Armigeri, anno D.M. 1703". The water issued through the mouths of two figures.

The tall early 18thc Allgood House behind the pant stood unaltered until it was demolished in 1878. The building on the right was the last remaining part of the row which had lined the west side of the Market Place (see page 13).

*plate 9*

*10*

The same area, with replacement late 19[th]c buildings. On the left is a passageway through Old Church to Meal Market. The building retains two old doorways and two blocked windows of the Allgood House.

*plate 10*

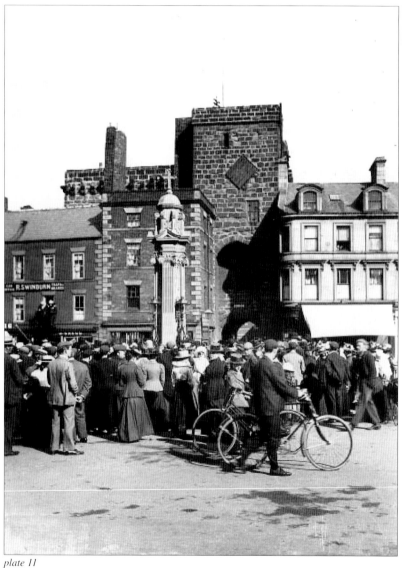

*plate 11*

*Left*
The formal handing over of the Market Cross and Fountain on 28th August 1901, on behalf of the family of the late Mr. W. A. Temperley, to Hexham Urban District Council.

---

*Inscription on*
*The Market Cross*
*and Fountain*

*O you who drink my cooling waters clear*
*Forget not the far hills from whence they flow*
*Where over fell and moorland year by year*
*Spring summer autumn winter come and go*
*With showering sun and rain and storm and snow*
*Where over the green bents forever blow*
*The four free winds of heaven ; where time falls*

*In solitary places calm and slow.*
*Where pipes the curlew and the plover calls,*
*Beneath the open sky my waters spring*
*Beneath the clear sky welling fair and sweet,*
*A draught of coolness for your thirst to bring,*
*A sound of coolness in the busy street.*

*Wilfrid Wilson Gibson*          *February 1901*

*plate 12*

*Left*
The row of buildings in 1832 which were built into the fabric of the Lady Chapel of the Abbey and demolished between 1841 and 1852.

*Below*
A wider view in 1810 of the shops, houses and inn that extended from the west end of Market Place to Market Street.

*plate 13*

*plate 14*

*Above*
The Queen's Arms Inn, on the corner of Market Place and Back Row, also known as Pudding Mews, c.1900. The upper floors were demolished in 1953.

**TO BREWERS AND OTHERS**

TO BE LET

And entered upon on May-day 1872
All that HOUSE and other conveniences, called the
GOLDEN LION INN in Hexham.
Mrs Stainthorpe, 12 Hencotes Street

*Hexham Courant*    April 1872

The Golden Lion was in Back Row

*Below*
Mrs Ethel Riley outside her general dealer's shop The Olde Corner House in 1932. The original bow-fronted windows of the mid 18$^{th}$c brick building can be seen. Her son converted it into a tobacconist and sweet shop in 1946.

*plate 15*

# The Abbey

*plate 16*

The mid 12<sup>th</sup>c Priory gatehouse from an 1814 engraving. The vaulting and central dividing wall were removed about 1820.

*plate 17*

*Above*
A 1780 illustration of the Abbey, without a nave, and the 1539 Carnaby buildings from the north west.

*Right*
The arms of Sir Reynold Carnaby, with the date 1539, are carved on a panel on the north wall of the Carnaby buildings. He was granted the buildings and land by Henry VIII at the dissolution of the priory in 1537.

*plate 18*

*plate 19*

*Left*
An ink-wash c.1778 showing the ornate doorway in the west wall of the chapter house vestibule. The beautiful doorway was blown down in a thunderstorm in 1819.

*Right*
The Abbey from the north in 1740. The 1670 Mercers' doorway was removed in 1869.

*Hexham Church*

*plate 20*

*plate 21*

An engraving of Hexham Abbey Church, 1815, by Luke Clennel.
The view is from the Lord of the Manor's garden, now the Abbey Grounds.

*Right*
An 1833 etching by T. Allom of the south transept of the Abbey.

*Below*
The ancient stone seat, known as the Frith Stool, was carved from a single sandstone block. It was the seat of the 7[th]c abbots and bishops and was also a seat of sanctuary. The sanctuary extended for an old mile (equal to 1.5 miles today) around the church. The names White Cross and Maiden Cross record the limits of the sanctuary. The northern most cross stood in the river Tyne, but the location of the southern cross is unknown.

*plate 22*

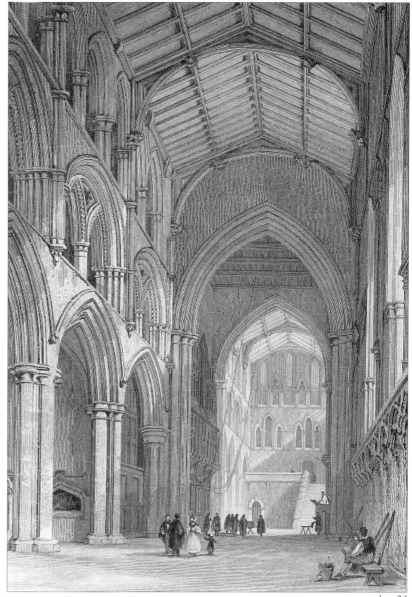

*plate 23*

*plate 24*

# Moot Hall

The Moot Hall, where the law-courts of Hexhamshire were held. The first floor contained the hall of justice, and the upper rooms were the bailiff's lodgings and store rooms. This 14[th]c building was the fortified gateway to the Archbishop's Palace with originally three sets of gates within the archway. The 18[th]c external stair on the east side, seen in this early illustration of 1778, conceals an earlier doorway.

HEXHAM.

A late 19<sup>th</sup>c painting of the east side of the Moot Hall.

*plate 25*

Joseph Johnson's ironmonger's shop on the east side of the Moot Hall, c.1905.

*plate 26*

22

plate 27

*Above*

The Stocks were where petty criminals were publicly confined and humiliated during medieval times.

*Left*

The Moot Hall c.1900. It ceased to be used as a courthouse after 1838 and was later used for storage and living accommodation. Selby Robson, a postman, was born there in 1890. The building was conveyed to the Lockhart Trust around 1910 for use as a museum, library or other public instition.

plate 28

# The Old Gaol

*plate 29*

An early pen-and-ink wash of the Old Gaol c.1778.

Built as a gaol with dungeons by the Archbishop of York in 1330, it served that purpose until 1824 when it was used to transact the business of the Manor of Hexham, then known as the Manor Office, until 1868.

*plate 30*

A late 19$^{th}$c photograph of the Manor Office.

The single-storey buildings, shown in plate 29, have been removed by this time and the roof has been extended over the projecting corbels. The Old Gaol now houses a museum and the Border History Library.

*Left*
The late 17th c doorway.

*Below*
The Old Grammar School c.1900
Founded by a Royal Charter of Queen Elizabeth on 29th June 1599, the Free Grammar School was carried on at first in private houses. This school building and a convenient house for the Master were built at the expense of the town and neighbourhood in 1684. It had one large schoolroom 48 x 18ft with dormitories over it for the boarders.

# The Old Grammar School

*plate 31*

plate 32

Queen Elizabeth Grammar School, Hallbankhead c.1885. When the
school closed in 1881, this building became a private residence.

*plate 33*

The Master and Assistant with the scholars. The Master's house and the caretaker's single-storey house are behind them. There is no window in the gable end of the school building beyond the houses so the photograph was probably taken before 1862 when the school was modernised.

The statutes ordain that the master shall be furnished in the Greek and Latin tongues; a catechism shall be taught weekly; grammar shall be securely taught; epistles shall be written weekly; orations written and recited; and there shall be a weekly exercise in versification; Latin to be spoken in school; no sword or dagger shall be worn.

*History of Hexham 1823*

28

# Hallstile Bank

*plate 34*

*Above*
Nos. 27 to 33; four houses designed by C.C.Hodges, architect, for Thomas Ellis which were built in 1888.

*Left*
Hallstile Bank c.1880, before Thomas Ellis had the houses built on the right-hand side. The house on the left with the plaque, now illegible, on the gable end was the 1830 Primitive Methodist Chapel. It closed for worship in 1863 and was later converted into two dwellings.

*plate 35*

*Left*
The left side of Hallstile Bank, before the Georgian houses (nos.18-22) were demolished in 1978. It was made a one-way street in 1967.

*Right*
Above no.18 stood this house and shop which were demolished in 1890. The shop sold penny pies and was celebrated for its gingerbread horses.

*plate 36*

plate 37

The garden with steps is on the site of the shop in plate 36. The late 17<sup>th</sup>c vaulted cellar may have belonged to an earlier building than Prospect House now above it.

*plate 38*

## Alms Houses

Work on these new almshouses was completed in December 1893, financed by a bequest from Henry King of Prospect House. The fine 17[th]c gateway was formerly part of a house in Fore Street. An earlier alms house stood in Battle Hill, but by 1812 it was in Hencotes. Records show that there had been an alms house in Hexham since at least the 16th century.

Received to the trustees of Hexham Turnpike Road One Years Interest of One Hundred pounds belonging to the Alms Houses in Hexham and due 6th Nov 1791

12th January 1792 Paid the above Sum to the Poor Widows in the Alms House as follows

| | |
|---|---|
| Eleanor Wilson | £1 . 5 . 00 |
| Barbara Cinnamon | £1 . 5 . 00 |
| Jane Bell | £1 . 5 . 00 |
| Jane Rochester | £1 . 5 . 00 |
| | £5 . 0 . 00 |

*fig. 2*

*Left and Below*
The front house facing Hallstile Bank was adapted for an aged couple or two elderly persons who agreed to live together. The four remaining cottages which face south each contained "a commodious living room (with fold-down bed), pantry and closet, together with necessary conveniences in the adjoining yard".

# *Fore Street*

*Left*

Red Lamp Hotel c.1900 at 12 Fore Street. The Turf Hotel, Blue Bell Inn, Sun Inn and White Hart Inn were also trading in Fore Street at this time. The White Hart name was transferred here when that inn closed in 1916 although it still retained the RED LAMP in the mosaic tiles in the doorway. It closed in 1973.

**Trades carried out in Fore Street in 1822**

*3 attorneys, 1 banker, 1 bookbinder, 6 boot & shoemakers, 1 butcher, 1 chemist, 1 glass & china dealer, 9 grocers, 3 inns, 2 joiners & cabinet makers, 8 linen & woollen drapers, 3 saddlers, 4 shopkeepers, 1 straw hat maker, 3 watch & clock makers, 1 wine, spirit & porter merchant and 1 spinning wheel maker.*

*fig. 3*

*plate 39*

plate 40

*Left*

Gibson & Son, 16&18 Fore Street c.1905. The pharmacy was founded by William Wilson Gibson in 1834. John Pattison Gibson (1838-1912), pictured below, succeeded his father in the business and was a well- respected photographer who won international awards for his pictures. He was also a keen archaeologist with an active interest in local Roman sites and in the history of the Abbey.

plate 41

*Left*
Arms of the City of London. John Pattison Gibsons's son John was admitted to the Freedom of the City of London in 1908 as a Freeman of the Worshipful Company of Spectacle Makers. His grandson J. Philip Gibson was also later admitted as a Freeman.

*Above*
The ornate carving was executed by Josephus Ceulemans, a Belgian refugee (one of 400 in Hexham in WW1) as an expression of gratitude to the Gibson family who provided meeting rooms and a library of French and Flemish books for the refugees. The left shield bears the letters JPG around the sun, necessary for photography, while the right shield shows JG around an eye, representing an optician.

*Left*
Gibson's shop c.1970.

*plate 42*

*plate 43*

*plate 44*

*"Sight-Testing conducted Daily at the Private Sight-Testing Rooms" 1914*

John Gibson was succeeded by his son J.Philip until the latter retired in 1978 and the shop closed. The shop front was recreated in the Science Museum in London and the fittings and fixtures were transferred there.

*Left*
An interior photograph of Gibson's Pharmacy.

*plate 45*

*Advertisements dating from 1886 to 1915
for shops in Fore Street*

## *Photographers*

There were at least four professional photographers in Hexham in the 1890s: J. P. Gibson & Son and T. H. McAllan in Fore Street, T. W. Milburn in Battle Hill and J. J. Gloag in Pearson's Terrace. J. P. Gibson and Son produced a large amount of local photographs, many of which have been reproduced in this book. They also sold a wide range of postcards.

NEW SERIES OF VIEWS OF

# Hexham and Neighbourhood

PUBLISHED BY

W. M. LISLE, Stationer & Bookseller,

The Library, Fore Street, HEXHAM-ON-TYNE.

**Containing 16 Views.     Price One Shilling.**

Also in Stock a Splendid Selection of Permanent Photographs of the District, Mounted and Unmounted.

*plate 46*

*Above*

W. M. Lisle's stationers and booksellers shop, like several other stationers, sold books of local photographs in addition to postcards.

*Left*

Carte de Visites were popular during the second half of the 19th century.

*Right*

T. H. McAllan was a music seller, stationer and instrument dealer in addition to being a photographer.

*plate 47a*          *plate 47b*          *plate 47c*

plate 48

The White Hart Hotel and gateway to the inn yard c.1890. It was an important inn and posting house where magistrates held petty sessions for Tynedale on the first Tuesday of every month. It was closed in 1916 and demolished in 1929. The archway was removed to Beaumont Street and given to the town by Mr Robb in 1919 as a war memorial to the Northumberland Fusiliers.

*plate 49*

Fore Street from Cattle Market in the 1890s

ESTABLISHED 1800.

## Hogarth & Co.,

Tea Dealers,
Family Grocers,
Italian Warehousemen,
and Provision Merchants,

✳ ✳ ✳

39, Fore Street,

HEXHAM.

Noted for High Class Provisions.

Fore Street from Cattle Market c.1905. On the extreme left is Robb's 1901 shop and on the far right is the White Hart Hotel. The sign for the Sun Inn can be seen further down the street at no. 36.

*plate 50*

*plate 51*

Boots the Chemist at 54-56 Fore Street c.1949. The double-fronted shop had previously been occupied by Low & Hare. In 1950 they moved to their present site at nos. 7 & 9. Robbs then took over this property.

Originally a Scottish lace trader from Fife. In 1818 William Robb registered his business as linen and woollen drapers at Goose Market, Hallgate. He built new shops in Fore Street in 1890 & 1901, and in 1960 brought all the departments together under one roof with an entrance from Priestpopple.

**ESTABLISHED 1818.**

# W̱ᴹ. ROBB & SON

High-class

| DRAPERS AND | HOUSE FURNISHERS. |
| SILK MERCERS. | REMOVERS. |

## HEXHAM-ON-TYNE.

| GENT.'S OUTFITTERS. | TAILORS. |
| DRESSMAKERS | MILLINERS. |

Boot and Shoe Dealers.

Every department of the business is fully and efficiently staffed and is under experienced control.

Estimates given free for whole or part Furnishing Removing, Storing, Repairing and Renovating.

*Special Mail Order Department for convenience of country clients.*

Addresses:— 2, 4, 35, 37 & 52, Fore Street, St. Mary's Chare, Hallgarth & Beaumont St., HEXHAM.

TELEPHONE: 21 P.O. TELEGRAMS: "ROBB, HEXHAM"

*plate 52*

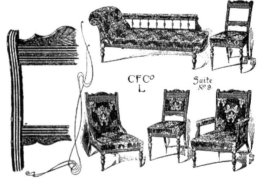

# WM. ROBB & SON,

## General Drapers & House Furnishers.

Before buying, call and inspect the large and varied Stock of

**BEDROOM SUITES, SITTING ROOM SUITES, SIDEBOARDS. KITCHEN FURNITURE a speciality.**

### SPECIMEN SUITE.

CFCº L

Suite Nº 9.

Extra Strong Frames, Upholstered in Saddlebags and Velvet, £6 : 6 : 0.

# Wm. Robb & Son, Hexham.

# Meal Market

*Right*
On the north side of Meal Market is the oldest house on the site of St. Mary's church for which there is any record.

*Below*
When the 17[th]c house was demolished in 1883, the decorative stone doorhead was rebuilt into West End Terrace by William Harrison.

OLD HOUSES, HEXHAM.

*plate 53*

45

# *Old Church*

*Left*
The shop of Hedley, cabinet maker, is to the left and next to it is the old Grapes Inn with a mounting block for horse riders; beyond that is Old Church. Dr. Joseph Parker D.D. was born in the next house in 1830. The house was demolished in 1904.

*Below*
Dr. Parker was ordained a Congregational minister. In 1874 he opened the City Temple in London and became President of the National Free Church Council. He was the author of 75 books including *The People's Bible*.

*plate 54*

*plate 55*

When the buildings were taken down in 1904 remains of the 13[th]c St. Mary's Church were revealed. Built on the site of St.Wilfrid's 8[th]c church, the medieval church was in a state of disrepair at the dissolution of the monasteries in 1537 so the Abbey then became solely the parish church. Later buildings incorporated the remains of St. Mary's, and the path through it became known as Old Church.

*plate 56*

# St. Mary's Chare

plate 57

St. Mary's Chare, commonly called Back Street, decorated for the 1910 Coronation of King George V.
In the background is Domenico Bonini's confectioner's shop in Meal Market.

*Right*
C.Fraser and E.Tyson, Mr Robert Colman's apprentices, 1920, at the warehouse in Back Row.

*Below*
Colman's upholstery shop c.1910 at 2 Back Street on the corner of Meal Market, seen here with Robert Colman and staff. He sold house furnishings, upholstery and offered motor car trimming services.

*plate 58*

*plate 59*

*plate 60*

The Grapes Inn 1899. This typical Victorian public house was erected on the site of a 16th century building. The coat of arms (left) are those of Thomas Lord Dacre, bailiff of Hexhamshire (1514-1532) during the most lawless period of Border conflict. They can be seen above the main entrance.

*plate 61*

*Left*
The advert for the Grapes Hotel, c.1900, offers "Good Accommodation for Cyclists; Stabling; Commodious Dining Room and Grill".

*Below*
An artist's impression of the back of the 16thc Grapes Inn. It was known as the Grapes & Barleycorn in the 1820s.

*plate 62*

*plate 63*

This is the view looking north along Back Street from the Old Grey Bull in Cattle Market;
the decorations are for King George V's Coronation in 1910.

*plate 64*

53

**"George & Dragon Inn"**
A DANCE will be held at Mr BELL'S
George and Dragon Inn on Friday, May 13<sup>th</sup> 1870

Tickets 6d each

*Hexham Courant*

The George and Dragon, seen here
c.1900, was formerly a coaching inn
with its yard behind. Closed in
1937, it is now a listed building.

# *Beaumont Street*

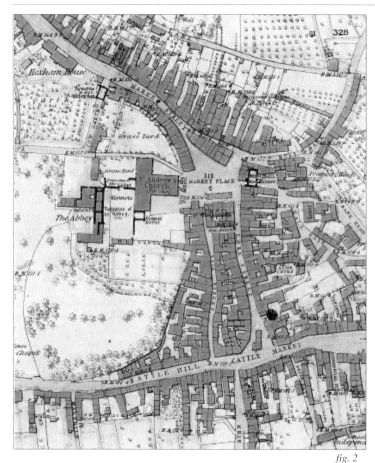

*fig. 2*

*fig. 3*

*Above*

The dark line on the 1860 map shows the extent of the former Priory grounds. Here they are the garden of the Lord of the Manor, whos house is called The Abbey.

*Right*

Here is the same area in 1896 after Beaumont Street had cut across the grounds. The street was made in 1866 to link the Market Place with Battle Hill. It was made at the expense of the Lord of the Manor and named Beaumont Street after him.

*Right*
A *Carte de Dance* for a Yeomanry Ball at Christmas.

*Below*
To administer the local agricultural trade, the Corn Exchange Company
was formed and by 1857 needed a permanent building for weekly markets.
Mr Beaumont offered land for a building to house the new limited company,
and later laid the foundation stone. When it opened in 1866 the Corn Exchange
occupied the central portion, the Town Hall with the Local Board of Health
the south wing, and Lambton's Bank the north wing.

*plate 64*

*plate 65*

*plate 67*

This view of Beaumont Street in 1886 shows the scaffolding for the building of the Wesleyan Methodist Chapel.

*Left*
Robert Short was a horse keeper and rolley man at the railway station. He led the first load of stone for the Town Hall. Mr Short was a much-respected member of the community, serving on the new Hexham Urban District Council and the Board of Health. He was also a representative on the workhouse Board of Guardians.

*Below*
Beaumont Street c.1890

*plate 68*

*Right*

Tom Scott, managing director of Hexham
Entertainment Company, stands beside a float
for the 1928 Hexham Carnival.

*Below*

In 1920 Hexham Entertainment Co. took over the
Town Hall and was granted a licence to use it as a
cinema; it became known as the Queen's Hall. The
Corn Exchange Company went into liquidation. The
Queen's Hall closed in 1976 and was bought by the
District Council and County Council. The new
Queen's Hall Art Centre was opened in 1983,
housing a theatre, county library and exhibition
rooms.

*Below Right*

A programme for an early film shown at the cinema.

*plate 69*

*plate 70*

*plate 71*

*plate 72*

*Left*

The Abbey Hotel c.1905. Opened in 1902 as a temperance hotel, it had 44 single bedrooms for male commercial travellers. At the rear an annexe housed coaches on the ground floor and horses were led up a ramp to the first floor stables. The name was changed to the Beaumont Hotel in 1953, when it became licensed.

MEMORIAL, HEXHAM.

*plate 73*

*Right*

The Benson Memorial, a statue by John Tweed, was erected in 1904 by public subscription. Col.Benson, born in 1861 at Allerwash, was a scientist. His death persuaded Kitchener to sue for terms with the Boers.

*plate 74*

The foundation stone laying of the Primitive Central Methodist Church on the old auction mart site on June 8th 1908.

plate 75

The Consecration Ceremony of the church on May 31ˢᵗ 1909. It closed for worship on 28ᵗʰ December 1952, when the congregation united with the Wesleyans. Members of the Community Church have worshipped here since 1993.

# *Abbey Grounds*

*Left*
The gates were presented in memory of his brother Col. G.E.Benson by T.W.Benson of Allerwash. By a generous contribution he enabled the town to acquire the Abbey Grounds, opened in September 1911, as a public park.

*plate 76*

*Right*
The opening ceremony in 1919 of the Northumberland Fusiliers War Memorial gateway in the Abbey Grounds. The gateway was originally sited at the White Hart Hotel in Fore Street (see page 40).

*plate 77*

# The Sele

*Right and Below*
The drinking fountain erected in 1899 on the Sele by the Abbey C. of E. Temperance Society as a memorial of Queen Victoria's Diamond Jubilee.

Inscription reads "KEEP THE PAVEMENTS DRY"

*Below*
The Abbey Grounds seen from Sele Walk. The bandstand was presented by Henry Bell, woolstapler and fellmonger, in 1912.

*plate 78*  63  *plate 79*

Sele Well                                        Hexham

*plate 80*

*Above*
The Sele Well c.1905. When the well was brought into working order in 1901 the water was said to be of superior quality to other public water supplies in the town.

*Right*
The northern boundary of the Sele, 1860, showing the Sele Well and the Selewell Bridge.

*fig. 4*

*plate 81*

*Left*
Children at the Sele
School in 1910. Built
in 1856 as a Subscription
School, it became a
Board School in 1874
and a Hexham Council
School in 1902.

To the left is part of the original 1856 school and to the right is the 1915 building.

*plate 82*

# *Market Street*

Market Street c.1890. This 17th century building had been demolished by 1900. Although in poor condition at the time of this photograph it had apparently been of good quality, with shutters made from carved oak. The barber's shop on the left was destroyed by fire in the 1920s. The doorway on the extreme right was a butcher's shop and still has the metal mesh ventilation panel above the door.

The sign on the wall above the doorway, second from right.

THIS HOUSE & SHOP
FOR SALE. or TO LET
*Apply to* MRS. BATY.
21 HALL STILE BANK

The inscription on the stone door-head.
*Praise to the only God of Heaven and only Creator*

SOLI . DEO . CAELI . AC . SOLI .
CREATORI . LAUS . IVLII . 15
AO . DNI . 1641
A
M    D

*plate 83*

Nos. 20 and 22 Market Street c.1900. These late 17<sup>th</sup>c buildings are some of the oldest surviving in Hexham.

*plate 84*

Hexham House c.1900 viewed from the south west.

*plate 85*

It was built in 1723 by the Revd. Thomas Andrewes, Lecturer at Hexham Abbey. The wings were added in the 19$^{th}$c. It remained a private residence until 1915, when it became the Hexham House School. It was sold in 1926 to be used as a public library but was instead made into Council Offices. The grounds were used as a bowling green and public park.

# Gilesgate

*Right*
Notice of properties in Gilesgate to be auctioned in 1830.

*Below*
1860 map showing Market Street and part of Gilesgate.

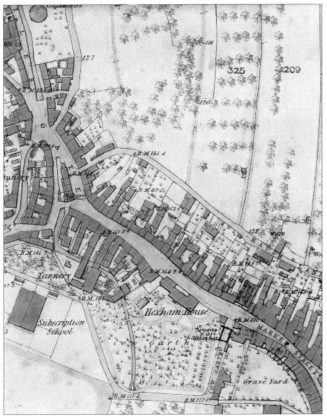

*fig. 5*

# TO BE SOLD
## by Auction,

AT THE HOUSE OF MR. BURN, THE WHITE HART INN, IN HEXHAM,

### ON TUESDAY THE 14th DAY OF DECEMBER NEXT,

*Between the Hours of four and six o'clock in the Afternoon,*

( IF NOT PREVIOUSLY DISPOSED OF BY PRIVATE CONTRACT OF WHICH DUE NOTICE WILL BE GIVEN, )

## Mr. John Rowland, Auctioneer,

THE FOLLOWING DESIRABLE

# PREMISES,

*Which will be put up together or in lots as may be agreed upon at the time of Sale. If the latter mode is adopted the Lots will be as Follow.—*

LOT I.—AN EXCELLENT

# DWELLING HOUSE,

SITUATED in Gilligate Street, Hexham, containing 11 Rooms with suitable Conveniences, and an extensive Tan Yard behind the same, in which there are 54 Tan Pits, 2 Drying Houses, a good Bark Mill and Loft, and a Ring Wheel, together with a Stable and Hay Loft, and all other requisite Conveniences, all of which are in good Repair. A small Rivulet which passes through the middle of the Yard affords a constant supply of Water without either trouble or expence.

LOT II.

## A Dwelling House,

Situated in Gilligate Street aforesaid, consisting of 4 Dwelling Rooms and a Hatter's Shop, with 2 Lofts above.

All the Premises are now in the Occupation of Mr. Edward Nicholson, at the yearly Rent of £70.

Mr. Richard Muse who resides on the premises will shew the same, and further Particulars may be known on application-at the Offices of Mr. CARR, Solicitor, Hexham

Hexham, November 10th, 1830.

*plate 86*

Old houses in Gilesgate seen from the north west c.1880.

*plate 87*

The door lintel, on the larger house
to the right, carried the inscription

HONI SOIT QUI MAL Y PENSE
W. S. E. .......ANO DOMAN 1638

The windows were mullioned, the door was iron studded
and a room on the left had an enormous fireplace about 10ft
wide. Tradition had it that it belonged to one of the county
families, many of whom had residences in Hexham. The
houses were demolished in 1885 to make way for Henry
Bell's wool warehouse, now the swimming pool.

*plate 88*

The same houses as shown opposite, photographed by J.P.Gibson from the south west.
He was awarded a diploma for this picture in 1886 by the Photographic Society of Philadelphia.

*plate 89*

*Above*

A composite advertisement picture entitled **TYNE GREEN WORKS**. To impress customers, it shows Henry Bell's fellmongers and artificial manure works at Tyne Green and in the foreground his new wool warehouse in Gilesgate. He started his business in 1840 and later employed forty assistants.

TELEPHONE P O Nº I & Nº III

TELEGRAPHIC ADDRESS,
BELLS HEXHAM.
ALSO AT
HARRABY GREEN,
CARLISLE.
TELEPHONE Nº 178

*Hexham Feb 6th 1925*

*M. Gibson*

*Beaumont House*

*Bought of* **HENRY BELL & SONS** L^{TD}

Fellmongers, Woolstaplers, Artificial Manure Manufacturers &c.

*Right*

The 1974 conversion of the 1885 wool warehouse into a swimming pool won a European Architectural Heritage Award.

*Right*
The shop of Miss Hannah Turnbull at 47 Gilesgate
decorated for the 1935 Silver Jubilee. The grocer's
and greengrocer's shop opened every day except
Christmas until it closed in 1999.

*Below*
The houses below the shop, nos. 51 and 53 were
removed under the 1934 Clearance Order. This is
now the site of Garland Place.

*plate 91*

*plate 90*

# Cockshaw

*Right*
Holy Island House c.1890. It was called *Holy* because it was a Roman Catholic Mass house in the days of the recusants, and *Island* because the Halgut Burn and Cockshaw Burn would join at the top of the street when they were in flood and surround the houses.

The date on the door lintel reads 1657 but the house is Elizabethan in style.

*Below*
Holy Island House 1989. The render has been removed from the upper storeys.

*plate 93*

*plate 92*

*plate 94*

Glovers Place c.1890. The thatched cottages were demolished and the burn was culverted in 1897 when the Skinners Arms was built. The first house beyond the burn at 1 Giles Place was the United Methodist Free Chapel from 1859 to 1862.

"A row of cottages by the side of the Cow Garth Burn, close to Holy Island, shows us what the poorer dwellings in Hexham were in days gone by. They are of one storey, and only contain one room each; but the dark thatch covered with moss, the whitewashed fronts, the tall red brick chimneys, and the burn running close in front make up a picture which to an artistic eye is more pleasing than a view of some nobleman's mansion" *Bulmer's Directory 1886.*

*plate 95*

This shows the windmill on what we now call Windmill Hill. In ruins by 1823, it had been used for grinding oak bark for use in the tanning industry.

*Above*
The doorhead of Priest's House

*plate 76*

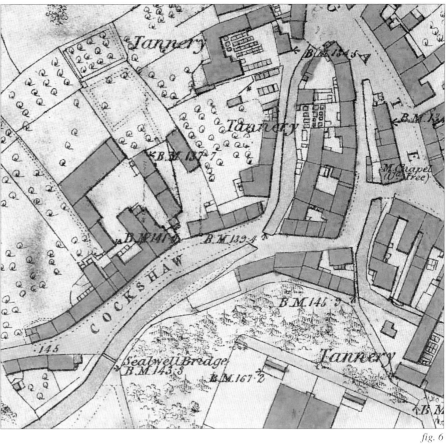

*fig. 6*

*Above*
A plan of the Cockshaw area in 1860. Note the rows of
tan pits where the tanneries are shown.

*Left*
10 Cockshaw, recently called the Priest's House, predates
the 1760 Roman Catholic Chapel which stood behind it.

# *House of Correction*

*Right*
The 1849 plan of the House of Correction, Tyne Green. Opened in 1784, it held petty criminals. It was closed in 1871, then sold and converted into houses.

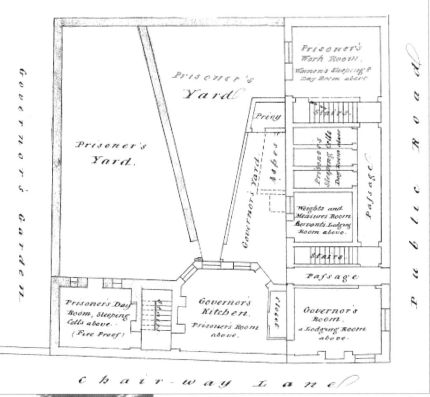

*fig. 7*

*Left*
The prisoners' day room with sleeping cells above is the only remaining building (see lower left corner of plan).

*plate 97*

Chareway Cottages 1895.

These cottages were converted from the Governor's residence when the House of Correction was closed. In 1891 Dorothy Hamilton, a widow, was running a grocer's shop from Chareway Cottages (see below). Her daughters Dorothy and Hannah, both dressmakers, and her son John, were living with her when this photograph was taken.

Mr & Mrs Taylor were running a shop here in the 1950s. Although the buildings were listed, all were demolished in 1972 except for the prisoners' day room (see plate 97).

*plate 98*

# *Tanneries*

*Right*

Hexham had a long history in the leather industry which was by far the largest employer in the 17th and 18th centuries. Tanning ceased to be of much importance by the late 19[th]c. This picture shows Smith Stobart's tannery over the Cockshaw Burn, one of the last remaining tannery buildings in Hexham. The tanners and shoe makers processed the heavy hides of cattle skins, making saddles, harness, shoes and belting.

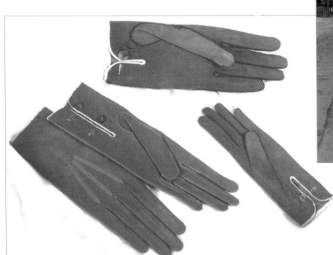

*plate 99*

*Left*

These are the type of gloves known as Hexham Tans. The skinners and glovers processed sheep and goat skins for clothing, particularly gloves; 23,504 dozen pairs of gloves were made in 1823.

*plate 100*

*Right*
Tan pits at one of only a few remaining tanneries in Hexham in the 1890s, by which time the leather industry was in decline. The men are soaking skins in a lime solution, only the beginning of a long and complex process involving lime, manure and oak bark solutions.

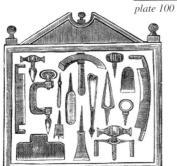

*18th century leather tools*

"In the Court Rolls of the 17th and 18th centuries, almost every other person named is a tanner, a glover, a cordwainer or a saddler"

*History of Northumberland*

|  | 1832 |
| --- | --- |
| Men and boys employed as leather dressers and glove-cutters | 71 |
| Boys employed as dusters | 40 |
| Women in Hexham and its vicinity employed in sewing | 1,000 |
| Total | 1,111 |
| Raw skins used annually | 80,000 |
| Skins of dressed leather imported annually | 18,000 |
| Total | 98,000 |

*fig. 8*

plate 101

This view c.1830 is towards the Abbey from Windmill Hill, looking over Cockshaw to the Sele where cattle are grazing. Note the bridge of 1793 over the River Tyne to the left of the picture.

# *Tyne Bridge*

*plate 102*

This illustration shows Smeaton's first bridge in 1778 after it had been damaged in construction. Gott's 1770 bridge had been destroyed in the dreadful flood of 1771. Wooler's later attempt in 1774 further west had been abandoned. Smeaton's bridge of 1780 was destroyed in half an hour on March 10th 1782 because of snow, then rain and a strong west wind. The present bridge, completed in 1793, has stood the test of time. It was Smeaton's design re-used and built by the County Surveyors, Thompson and Johnson, on very different foundations, as advised by Robert Mylne.

*plate 103*

*Above*
Skaters on the frozen River Tyne
in February 1929.

*Right*
Tyne Bridge from the south bank c.1900. This
shows the huge cutwaters on the west face of the
1793 bridge, before the carriageway was widened
in 1967.

*plate 104*

*plate 105*
The boat landing at Tyne Green near the site of the Low Ford c.1900.

Until 1793 the only ways of crossing the Tyne at Hexham were by the Low Ford and the East Boat Ferry, or by the West Boat Ferry which was at Warden. Many people died when crossing the river in severe weather.

*Bridge End*

plate 106

Bridge End Brewery from the north bank c.1900 of the Tyne. Founded in 1773, it was said in 1823 to be "of yet greater magnitude" than the very considerable brewery in Priestpopple. It closed in 1874 and the Old Brewery premises were sold by auction.

*plate 107-*

*Left*
Notice of the auction in 1856 of the brewery when it belonged to Donkin, Elstob & Co. When it was bought, re-opened and remodelled by Ayton & Co. it employed twenty-two men and six horses.

There were several small breweries trading during the 19thc but only two large scale breweries: Bridge End Brewery (left) and Northumberland Brewery at 25 Priestpopple.

*Right*
John Miller & Son of Market Street, Bell & Riddle of Market Place, Robert Hamilton of Gilesgate and John Thomas Trotter of Market Place were all selling bottled mineral and aerated water in the 19th and early 20th centuries.

John T. Trotter of the Black Bull at the top of Hallstile Bank and John Miller were also wine, spirit, ale and porter merchants.

*plate 108*

*plate 108*

*Left*
A group of workers
outside the Great
Northern Dye Works
c.1900

A dye works was established c.1850 by John
Fenwick & Son near the old brewery. The plentiful
supply of water and extensive area of bleaching
ground made it an ideal site for the dyeing and
laundry business.

*Right*
Bridge End House, built between 1800-1810, is
very Scottish in style. It was the home of the
Fenwick family and later of Walter Chapman, the
managing director of Fenwick's, until 1930 when
the company ceased trading.

Fenwick's Bridge End Works c.1900.

*Left*
The ironing room where the workers seem to be using steam or gas-heated irons.

*plate 109*

*Right*
Men in the dyeing room. Clothes were sometimes redyed to improve their appearance.

*plate 110*

*plate 111*

Bridge End Cottages with smithy c.1890; they faced towards the River Tyne.

*Facing Page*
**The Smithy, Hexham Bridge End** was painted by Ralph Hedley in 1885.
The blacksmith is John Lee who is listed in Bulmer's Directory of 1886
as "horse shoer and general smith".

*plate 112*

# Railway Station

The first section of the railway line was opened to passengers from Hexham on March 9th 1835. It went as far as Blaydon. When it opened from Redheugh Quay to Carlisle Canal Basin on 18th June 1838, there was an uninterrupted line of 60 miles. The Grand Opening Ceremony was a "display unequalled perhaps in the history of railways". At first the trains ran on the right-hand line but, to conform with the rest of the N.E.Railway, it changed to the left-hand line in 1864.

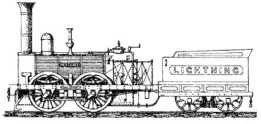

*fig. 9*

" Lightning", built in 1836/37, was one of the first locomotives to be used on the Newcastle to Carlisle line.

*plate 113*

The Depot, Hexham Station 1836

*Below*
Mr Bacon Grey was responsible for a serious delay when he took out an injunction against the use of steam locomotives crossing land at Styford.

*Below Right*
A paper published in 1825 on the advantages to be derived from a railway, and also a report on a proposed canal between Newcastle & Carlisle.

*fig. 10*

"Comet" the first locomotive used at the opening of Hexham Railway Station.

# NEWCASTLE
## AND
# CARLISLE
# RAILWAY.

**THE DIRECTORS of the NEWCASTLE UPON TYNE AND CARLISLE RAILWAY have the liveliest Satisfaction in announcing that Mr Bacon Grey, yielding his legal Rights to the Feeling of the Public, in a Manner highly honourable to himself, has abandoned his Injunction by which the Company is restrained from using Locomotive Engines, and has withdrawn his Opposition to the Bill now before Parliament.**

In Consequence of this satisfactory Arrangement the Use of the Railway will be resumed on **WEDNESDAY FIRST**, from which Day the Company's Trains of Carriages will set out at the Hours formerly announced, viz.:—From Blaydon and Hexham each Day at 8 and 11 o'Clock in the Forenoon, and **2** and **5** o'Clock in the Afternoon. For the present the Trains will not travel on Sundays.

## MATTHEW PLUMMER,
### CHAIRMAN.
*Newcastle upon Tyne, 4th May,* **1835.**

Mitchells Printers Newcastle.

*plate 114*

---

**Observations**

ON

## CANALS AND RAIL-WAYS,

ILLUSTRATIVE OF THE

AGRICULTURAL AND COMMERCIAL ADVANTAGES TO BE
DERIVED FROM AN IRON RAIL-WAY,

*Adapted to common Carriages,*

BETWEEN

NEWCASTLE, HEXHAM, AND CARLISLE;

WITH

ESTIMATES OF THE PRESUMED EXPENSE,
TONNAGE, AND REVENUE.

BY THE LATE WILLIAM THOMAS, ESQ.

ALSO, SECOND EDITION,

**Report**

OF

BARRODALL ROBERT DODD, ESQ.

CIVIL ENGINEER, &c.

ON

## A PROPOSED NAVIGABLE CANAL,

*Between Newcastle and Hexham ;*

WITH

**APPENDIX,**

CONTAINING REMARKS ON THE GREAT UTILITY OF A
PROPOSED JUNCTION CANAL, OR RAIL-WAY,

*Uniting Newcastle upon Tyne and Carlisle with Liverpool, Manchester,
Hull, Derby, Sheffield, Birmingham, Bristol, and London.*

**Newcastle upon Tyne :**

PRINTED BY G. ANGUS, SIDE, AND SOLD BY W. HEATON, SANDHILL, AND J. FINLAY,
MOSLEY STREET ; ALSO BY LONGMAN AND CO., LONDON ; RAY, LIVERPOOL ;
CONSTABLE AND CO., EDINBURGH, &c. &c.

1825.

*fig. 11*

### NEWCASTLE-UPON-TYNE AND CARLISLE RAILWAY.

TIMES OF DEPARTURE OF THE TRAINS ON AND AFTER OCTOBER 1st, 1845.

**GOING WEST THROUGH THE WEEK.**

| TRAINS | Leave Newcastle | Leave Gateshead | Leave Blaydon | Leave Stocksfield | Leave Hexham | Leave Haydon Bridge | Leave Haltwhistle | Leave Rose Hill | Leave Milton | Arrive at Carlisle |
|---|---|---|---|---|---|---|---|---|---|---|
| 1. Morning | 7 0 | | 7 15 | 7 45 | 8 13 | 8 38 | 9 5 | 9 20 | 9 45 | 10 15 |
| 2. Morning (Mail) | 10 0 | 9 50 | 10 15 | 10 45 | 11 13 | 11 38 | 12 5 | 12 20 | 12 45 | 1 15 |
| 3. Noon (Short) | 12 0 | | 12 15 | 12 46 | 1 18 | Arrives at Haydon Bridge at 2 o'clock. | | | | |
| 4. Afternoon | 2 0 | 1 50 | 2 15 | 2 45 | 3 13 | 3 26 | 4 20 | 4 35 | 5 15 | 5 15 |
| 5. Afternoon | 4 0 | 3 50 | 4 15 | 4 46 | 6 18 | 6 43 | 6 15 | 6 30 | 7 0 | 7 30 |
| 6. Evening | 6 45 | 6 35 | 7 0 | 7 30 | 7 58 | 8 23 | 8 50 | 9 5 | 9 30 | 10 0 |

**GOING WEST ON SUNDAYS.**

| | | | | | | | | | | |
|---|---|---|---|---|---|---|---|---|---|---|
| 1. Morning (Mail) | 9 45 | | 10 0 | 10 30 | 10 58 | 11 23 | 11 50 | 12 5 | 12 30 | 1 0 |
| 2. Afternoon | 5 0 | | 5 15 | 5 45 | 6 13 | 6 38 | 7 5 | 7 20 | 7 45 | 8 15 |

**GOING EAST THROUGH THE WEEK.**

| TRAINS | Leave Carlisle | Leave Milton | Leave Rose Hill | Leave Haltwhistle | Leave Haydon Bridge | Leave Hexham | Leave Stocksfield | Leave Blaydon | Arrive at Gateshead | Arrive at Newcastle |
|---|---|---|---|---|---|---|---|---|---|---|
| 1. Morning | 5 45 | 6 20 | 6 40 | 6 55 | 7 20 | 7 45 | 8 10 | 8 45 | 9 5 | 9 0 |
| 2. Morning (Short) | From Hexham only. | | | | 9 30 | 10 0 | 10 23 | | | 10 50 |
| 3. Morning | 9 0 | 9 35 | 9 55 | 10 10 | 10 35 | 11 0 | 12 0 | 12 30 | 2 55 | 2 55 |
| *4. Afternoon (Mail) | 12 5 | 12 30 | 12 45 | 1 0 | 1 25 | 1 45 | 2 10 | 2 40 | 3 0 | 2 55 |
| 5. Afternoon | 4 15 | 4 50 | 5 10 | 5 25 | 5 50 | 6 15 | 6 48 | 7 15 | 7 35 | 7 30 |
| 6. Evening | 7 0 | 7 30 | 7 47 | 8 5 | 8 30 | 8 53 | 9 15 | 9 45 | 10 5 | 10 0 |

**GOING EAST ON SUNDAYS.**

| | | | | | | | | | | |
|---|---|---|---|---|---|---|---|---|---|---|
| 1. Morning (Mail) | 9 0 | 9 35 | 9 55 | 10 10 | 10 35 | 11 0 | 11 25 | 12 0 | | 12 15 |
| 2. Afternoon | 5 0 | 5 35 | 5 55 | 6 10 | 6 35 | 7 0 | 7 25 | 8 0 | | 8 15 |

* N.B.—This Train will not call at Scotby, How Mill, or Low Row.

A Train will leave Newcastle Station for Blaydon every Evening, (Sundays excepted,) at a quarter before five o'clock, and return from Blaydon for Newcastle at a quarter-past five. And for the convenience of people attending Carlisle Market, a Train will leave Milton Station every Saturday Morning at half-past eight o'clock.

FARES.—(For the whole Distance between Newcastle and Carlisle) 1st Class, 11s.; 2nd Class, 8s. 6d.—Children, under Two Years of Age, Free; above Two, and under Ten, Half Price.

Parties riding inside their own Carriage, to pay First Class Fares; parties riding outside their own Carriages, to pay Second Class Fares. Goods and Parcels conveyed with Safety and Dispatch, and at moderate Rates.

Railway Office, Forth, Newcastle-upon-Tyne, Oct. 1st, 1845.     JOHN ADAMSON, Secretary.

*Newcastle: Printed at the Journal Office, by John Hernaman.*

*fig. 12*

A timetable for the line to Carlisle dated October 1st 1845.

*Right*
An etching entitled "The First Train leaves Hexham Station on the Opening of the Newcastle to Hexham railway in 1835".

Comfort in travelling varied considerably. First-class coaches provided excellent facilities whilst second-class coaches were open-sided. Second and third-class passengers were dependant on the weather for their comfort, the latter were seated in open wagons or on long benches fixed to carriage roofs.

*plate 115*

*Right*
Two of the four railway cottages at Warden c.1890.

*Below*
A steam train from Riccarton Junction, c.1940, crossing the Border Counties Railway Bridge over the Tyne just below Warden. The bridge was severely damaged in a storm in 1948. Temporary repairs kept the line going until the passenger service was withdrawn in 1956. The bridge was demolished in 1960.

*plate 116*

*plate 117*

*plate 118*

*Above*

In this 1890 view of Hexham from the railway bridge, the
town is dominated by the medieval Abbey and Moot Hall
and Hallstile Bank climbs steeply to the Market Place.
Although buildings have been altered, the road alignment is
still the same today. It is unusual to see so many people in an
early photograph. They are carefully posed with no movements
to blur the long exposure time needed for the plate negatives.

*Right*

A view of the railway station from the south c.1905.

*plate 117*

# Nurseries

Robert Hunter was listed as a nursery and seedsman in 1794 so we know that gardeners and nurserymen were trading in the town by at least the late 18[th]c. Pigot's Directory of 1822 listed fourteen gardeners and seedsmen. In 1886 Bulmer's Directory listed two nurseries and eighteen market gardeners and said that they were *"more flourishing and prosperous than heretofore. The nurseries, indeed, form one of the attractions of the town, and are visited by thousands during the summer season"*.

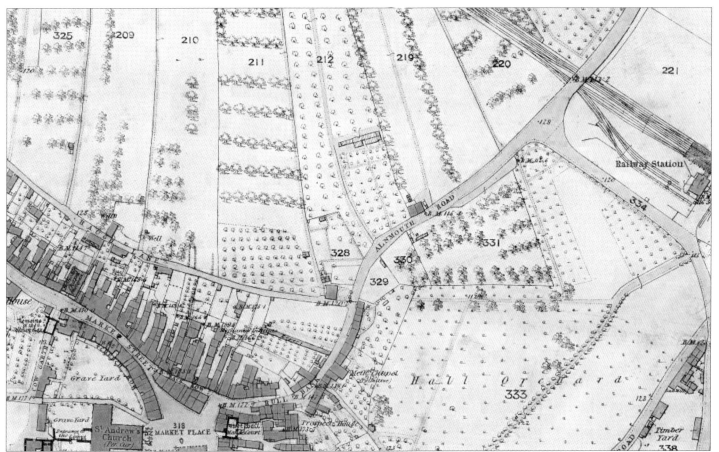

The 1860 map shows large areas of the land set out as market gardens or orchards.

*fig. 13*

*plate 120*

The Robson Nurseries were taken over by William Fell & Co. in 1879. The nurseries were at Wentworth, Fellside and Hudshaw, and covered some fifty acres.

**WANTED**, a MAN to take charge of a garden and also to attend to one or more Cows, Pony, and Carriage, an elderly man without children preferred. Apply to Mr. Ralph Robson, Nursery and Seedman. 11th April 1874      *Hexham Courant*

William Fell's nursery at Wentworth c.1900

*plate 121*

*plate 122*

Staff and workers at the Leazes Nursery of Joseph Robson & Son, c.1890, a long established firm dating back to at least 1822.

Wear's timber yard c.1900.

*plate 123*

William Wear & Co., timber merchants, had their Tyne Saw Mill in Orchard Place. The timber yard closed in the mid 1930s and is now the site of Matthew Charlton builders' merchants.

# Workhouse

*Right*
The Poor Law Act of 1601 made parishes
responsible for the poor. In 1823 a *poor-house*
was situated near the head of Priestpopple. Under
the new Act of 1834 a Poor-Law Union Workhouse,
seen in this 1860 map, was built at Peth Head. It
had room for 330 inmates. The yards between the
buildings gave space for exercise and kept men,
women and children separate. It was enlarged
over the years and several acres of land for new
buildings or for use as farmland were purchased.

Workhouse site in 1860                                    *fig. 14*

*Left*
The south side of one of the 19[th]c buildings
which now faces the road to Corbridge which
was re-aligned in 1931, separating the children's
home and school from the main workhouse
block. Some buildings had to be demolished.

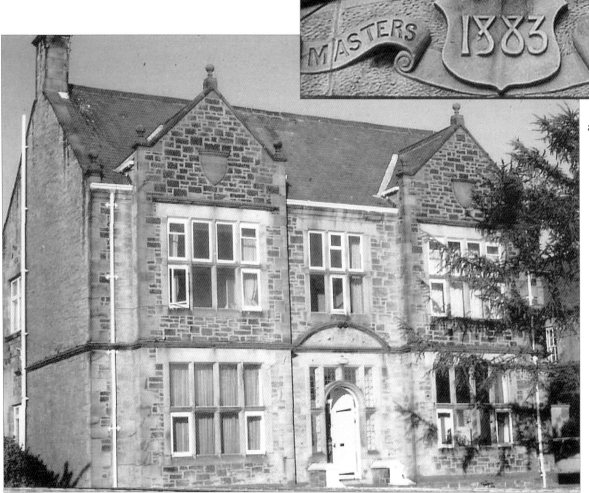

Carved stone detail above doorway of the Master's house.

*Left*
The Master's House, Hexham Workhouse

In 1883 extensive alterations and additions were made, including a new dining hall and kitchens, a porter's lodge, new cells for vagrants and, seen here, a house for the Master. The workhouse closed in 1939. The inmates were dispersed to Alnwick, Berwick or Morpeth Institutions. The buildings became part of Hexham Emergency Hospital.

**TREAT TO WORKHOUSE CHILDREN**

Yesterday, by kindness of Mrs Waddilove, Beacon Grange, the Wizard of the North, Mr George Robson, of Liverpool, gave two hours entertainment to the children of Hexham Workhouse, which greatly delighted his juvenile audience.

12th December 1874                    *Hexham Courant*

# Auction Marts

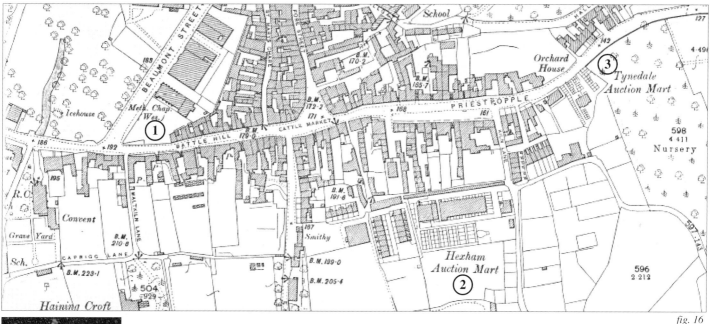

fig. 16

*Above*

The 1896 map shows the sites of (1) William Cook's mart of 1870, (2) his new mart of 1888, and (3) Tynedale Auction Mart.

*Left*

William Cook (1821-1900) began auctioning stock at the field on the corner of Battle Hill and Beaumont Street in 1870. The 1902 Abbey Hotel and the 1909 Central Methodist Church were later built on this site.

plate 124

### HEXHAM NOVEMBER FAIR

The last important fair of the year in this district, and one that has always been greatly looked forward to with very great interest by the agriculturists and job-seekers of the neighbourhood, took place on Wednesday last. The spot selected for the holding of the fair was a conveniently sized field at the head of Hencotes, the same in fact that has latterly been set apart by the authorities for this description of gathering. From an early hour on the previous evening stock began to arrive on the ground, and continued to be imported until about eleven o'clock on the following morning, when the business transactions of the day commenced.

16th November 1864       *Hexham Herald*

*plate 125a*

*plate 125b*

*Above*

The Iveson brothers from Hawes, William (1852-1922)
and Thomas (1854-1934), joined William Cook in 1879.
William Cook's home at 14 Hencotes became the office
for William Cook & Co.

*Right*

Mart employee Joe Philipson with his wife Mary and
children outside their home at Mart House, Wanless Lane,
in 1906. The house was demolished in 1979 when the
auction mart was extended.

*plate 126*

*plate 127*

*Left*

"Lancey" Dobbison, with his Border collie, was typical of the drovers who moved cattle and sheep between farms and markets. A retired blacksmith and Crimean War veteran, he was one of the few survivors of the Charge of the Light Brigade at Balaclava.

*Below*

A sale ring at Hexham Mart c.1944. When William Cook died in 1900, Hexham Auction Mart Company was formed. They later took over Tynedale Auction Mart and by the end of the 20thc had moved to Tyne Green.

*plate 128*

*plate 129*

Pupils outside the main entrance to the new Queen Elizabeth Grammar School c.1910.

plate 130

*Above*
Queen Elizabeth Grammar School at South Park, Fellside, was formally opened on November 2nd 1910. Classrooms were provided for 120 boys and 120 girls. This building became part of Hexham Middle School when Queen Elizabeth High School opened in 1965.

*Right*
The interior of the new school hall.

plate 131

*plate 132*
A smart pony with trap outside the premises of T.Swinburn, family grocer, at 20 Priestpopple c.1900.

*plate 133*

Carruthers Royal Hotel on the north side of Priestpopple 1902. Known as the Low Grey Bull and as the New Grey Bull in the mid-19[th]c, David Carruthers took over and renovated the inn in 1886. He renamed it the Royal Hotel, when it was listed as a commercial hotel and posting house.

plate 134

Priestpopple 1883, looking east, with Robert Welch's "Hair Cutting, Shaving & Shampooing Saloons" on the left. His shop was previously in Fore Street. Later, Robert's daughter also had a hairdressing business on these premises.

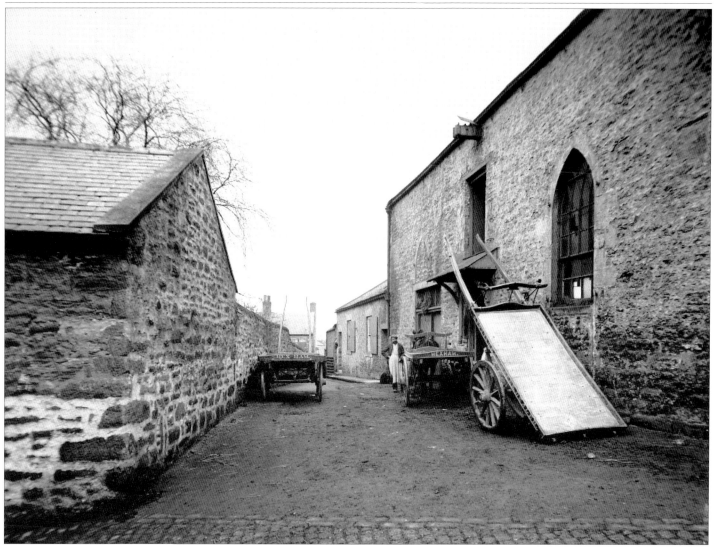

*plate 135*

The Ebenezer Chapel, The Fold, Broadgates c.1890. This independant chapel was opened on May 16th 1790, with a gallery added in 1812. The chapel was closed in 1869 when the members moved to the new Congregational Church in Hencotes. The Chapel was converted into a seed warehouse and then to a steam corn mill. The building is still standing and is known as Broadgates House.

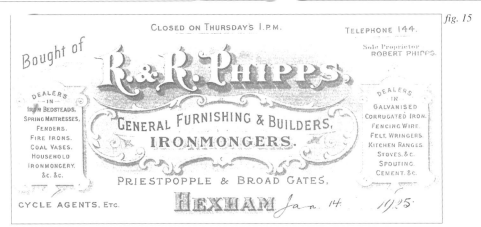

*fig. 15*

*Right*
The shop of R.Phipps, ironmongers, decorated for the Diamond Jubilee of Queen Victoria in 1897. The business traded from the late 19th c until the building was demolished in the 1960s.

*Below*
A window display c.1930.

*plate 136*

*plate 137*

*plate 138*

*Above*
The fruiterer's and florist's shop of
J.Holliday, 1901, at 2 Priestpopple.

*Right*
No. 4 Priestpopple c.1900. This
building was built as a bank by
Hodgkin Barnett & Co. in 1899 and
through the years has housed various
banks including Lloyds, North Eastern
Banking Co., Bank of Liverpool,
Martins Bank and now Barclays.

*plate 139*

*Below*
No.2 Priestpopple, to the left of what is now Barclays Bank, was built in 1895 for Lambton & Co. Lloyds took over Lambton's Bank in 1908 and moved from no.4 to no.2 Priestpopple.

*Above*
The Lambton & Co. carved wall plaque above the entrance to Lloyds bank. Lambton's were one of the first banks in the town and were trading in Fore Street in 1822.

*plate 140*

*plate 141*

*plate 142*

*Above*

Looking west from Cattle Market up Battle Hill c.1900. The building on the right, was built in 1896 for the Carlisle City & District Bank. Later that year it became the London City & Midland Bank and by 1999 it had become the HSBC Bank.

*Right*

White & Son, confectioners and caterers, on the opposite side of the road, at 13 Cattle Market c.1900.

plate 144

plate 143

*Above*
The lavishly ornamented London & Midland Bank of 1896 is at the junction of Fore Street and Cattle Market. Cherubs hold up this red sandstone swag on the north side which carries a lively decoration of contemporary coins of the realm.

*Left*
The buildings previously on this site were demolished in 1893.

# *Eastgate*

*plate 145*

The view down Eastgate towards Cattle Market c.1890. The smithy of J.J. Amos is on the right.

The thatched premises of John Joseph Amos, blacksmith and horse shoer c.1890. He also had a yard in Priestpopple where he built carts, dog-carts and rolleys. He is not listed in 1896, as by then his premises had been taken over by Joseph Beeby.

A second smithy in Eastgate in 1886 was owned by John Ward. His widow, Jane, continued in the business, being listed as the owner in 1896.

*plate 146*

*plate 147*

*Left*
Shield Close Cottages, Fellside, c.1890. During the late 19[th]c John W.Barker and Joseph Wilkinson lived at Shield Close.

*Below*
Middle Shield was built c.1710. The Lobley family ran a lodging house there in the late 19[th]c. John Elliott, farmer, was recorded as living there in 1879 and 1886, and Thomas Carr, also a farmer, was living there in 1896.

**MIDDLE SHIELD,**
For Sale by Public Auction in The Town Hall
28th November 1871
The above property comprises a Substantial DWELLING HOUSE of nine rooms, a large and productive GARDEN in front, a COTTAGE of two rooms, with Byre, Stable and other necessary Out-buildings, with about TWENTY THREE ACRES OF FREEHOLD LAND.
*Hexham Courant*                    25th November 1871

*plate 148*

*Right*
High Shield, Dipton Mill Road, was built by the mid 17ᵗʰc, extended in the early 18ᵗʰc, then given a new doorway in 1770.

Whilst solicitor, Thomas William Welford, was living at High Shield in 1886, a farm manager, John Roddam, was living in a separate house at the same address.

By 1898 Miss Welford had opened the High Shield House School for "daughters of gentlemen".

*plate 149*

*Left*
This old tannery building is just above High Shield. Skins and hides were dried in it for the leather and glove-making industries.
It was converted into a house c.1980.

*plate 150*

*120*

*plate 151*

St. Wilfrid's was built by Richard Gibson, an attorney, in the 1860s. His son Jasper lived there until his death in 1917. In 1919 Hexham War Memorial Committee purchased it from his widow with money raised by public subscription and fund-raising events. It was opened by Prince Henry, later Duke of Gloucester, on 29th September 1921 as a cottage hospital, to commemorate the men of Hexham who had laid down their lives in the war. When its closure was announced, plans were made to purchase the building and make it a Care Centre but, despite strong local disapproval, it was sold in 1995 and demolished to make way for commercial housing.

Eastgate c.1890.
Previously it was known as
Skinners Burn or sometimes
as Bone Street.

In 1822 it was the setting for
several industries: John Pattison
and Matthew Ward, blacksmiths;
William Hall, cartwright; John
Ridley, glove manufacturer;
William Wilson, joiner & cabinet
maker; William Hammel,
perfumer & hairdresser; William
Watson, tailor & habit maker.

*plate 152*

# *Battle Hill*

Priestpopple from W., Hexham

*plate 153*

The view from Battle Hill towards Cattle Market c.1910, with cattle being walked to the mart. The landlady of the Old Grey Bull in 1822 was Ann Charlton. In 1886 it was known simply as the Grey Bull Inn and Posting House, with Thomas Bell as landlord. James Oliver ran the inn in 1896, whilst Thomas Oliver & Sons were the licencees when this photo was taken. The inn closed in 1990 and was converted to shops with flats above.

*plate 154*

This picture of the painting and paperhanging shop and the Bee Hive Inn was painted by the owner John Guthrie in 1862, although in 1860 the old inn was actually called the Royal Oak. The premises were demolished and rebuilt in 1882 and renamed the Criterion. Thomas Hutchinson was the manager in 1880s.

*Right*
John Guthrie, in the tall hat, and his men photographed at his painting, paperhanging and glazing business c.1886. In addition to owning the Criterion and the decorating business, John Guthrie was also the licensee of the Sun Inn in Fore Street and the Tanners Arms in Gilesgate.

*plate 155*

*Left*
The corner of Eastgate and Battle Hill c.1900.

Battle Hill Post Office occupies the Eastgate side of the building whilst the Criterion Inn entrance is on Battle Hill.

*plate 156*

*plate 157*

This view westwards up Battle Hill, c.1910, suggests a more peaceful pace of life than ours today. On the right is Mrs Catherine Jameson's grocery shop at street level with dining and tea rooms behind and above it.

*plate 158*

H.P.Rose c.1905.  Mr Rose, whose assistant in seen here, traded as a ladies' and gentlemens' tailor from 5 Battle Hill. In 1914 he advertised "Estimates given for Motor and Carriage Liveries. Riding Breeches a Speciality". In the 1920s and 1930s he traded from St.Mary's Chare as well as this shop. When the shop closed in the 1960s the fabric swatches, patterns and buttons from the liveries of the large estates in the neighbourhood, which he had supplied, were still in stock. In 1939 Barclays Bank opened new premises, incorporating this shop.

plate 159

*Left*
At the top of Battle Hill was the Primitive Methodist Central Church shown on the left, and to the right the 1863 United Presbyterian Church. This was taken down in 1954 to provide a site for the Post Office. John Pattison Gibson, Chemist, archaeologist, and photographer, lived during the late 19thc at 1 Battle Hill Terrace, seen here on the right above the hooded archway. He and his wife Elizabeth brought up five daughters and two sons here. Their elder son John went in to the family business. The younger, Wilfrid Wilson Gibson, became a successful writer, well known nationally as one of the Dymock poets. He wrote the poem below and also the poem which is inscribed on the 1901 pant in the Market Place.

---

**NORTHUMBERLAND**

*Heatherland and bent-land –*
*Black land and white,*
*God bring me to Northumberland,*
*The land of my delight.*

*Land of singing waters,*
*And winds from off the sea,*
*God bring me to Northumberland,*
*The land where I would be.*

*Heatherland and bent-land,*
*And valleys rich with corn,*
*God bring me to Northumberland,*
*The land where I was born.*

W. W. Gibson                    1918

---

*fig. 16*

# *Hencotes*

*plate 160*

A view looking west along Hencotes c.1900, showing the 1869 Congregational Church which was demolished in 1967.
Further down the road, on the left, is the turning into St. Cuthbert's Terrace.

*plate 161*

*Right*
The staff outside the
greengrocer's shop of John
Winter at 15 Hencotes c.1910.

*Left*
Hencotes looking to the
east from Temperley
Place c.1910.

*plate 162*

*130*

St. Andrew's School

*plate 163*

**ST. WILFRID'S ROAD**
**PRIVATE SCHOOL FOR GIRLS**
MISS WILSON RESUMED her SCHOOL after holidays,
On Thursday 2nd May 1901. Special attention is
Given to French, German, and Music
Preparations made for Examinations
Prospectus on application
*Hexham Courant*                    July 13th 1901

**BATTLE HILL SCHOOL, HEXHAM**
Headmaster - CHAS. J. ROGERSON
Second Master, G. F. NIGHTINGALE
Assisted by an efficient Staff of Resident and
Non-Resident Masters
Pupils are prepared for Professional or
Commercial pursuits
Large Playground and Gymnasium
Prospectus on application
Next Term, TUESDAY, September 22nd

St Andrew's School was here at Burncroft from 1929.
By 1934 it had moved to Orchard Gap, Allendale Rd.
The Principal, Mrs Mary Allen, had opened the school
by 1925 in Battle Hill. Burncroft was a Day and
Boarding School for Girls, with a preparatory class for
boys where children were prepared for Oxford Locals,
Music, Elocution and R.D.S. Exams. In the grounds were
shrubberies, kitchen and ornamental gardens, an orchard
and tennis lawn. At the turn of the century there were 10
other private schools in Hexham, ranging in size from 8
to 48 pupils.

*plate 164*

The Convalescent Home, Hextol Court, seen here c.1910, was opened in 1893 for the Cathedral Nurse and Loan Society of Newcastle. It was a hospital in the 1914-1918 war for invalid soldiers and sailors. From 1933 it was The Nursery for Unfortunate Children from birth to 5 years old who were homeless. After World War II, when it had been used by the Ministry of Defence, it was converted into flats.

# West End

plate 165

Edward Robson is standing to the left
of his recently built butcher's shop at
Burncliffe, December 1898.

# *The Hydro*

plate 166

Tynedale Hydropathic Establishment was opened in 1879, on ground adjoining the private residence Westfield House, which was built in the 1850s, seen here on the left. The Mansion stood in 20 acres of grounds, set out with shrubberies near the house. In 1896 the Hydro offered Turkish and Electric Baths to the outside public as well as to residents. From 1941 it was used as a Children's Sanitorium, but by 1950 it had become the Northern Counties College of Domestic Science, and later a teacher training college. The building has been part of the Queen Elizabeth High School since 1974.

For over 60 years The Hydro was a popular venue for holidays as well as for afternoon tea dances and dinner dances.

TELEGRAPHIC ADDRESS – "HYDRO. HEXHAM."

NAT. TELEPHONE No O88

P.O. TELEPHONE No 38.

TYNEDALE HYDROPATHIC MANSION, HEXHAM, NORTHUMBERLAND.

*March 23rd. 1*

*plate 168*

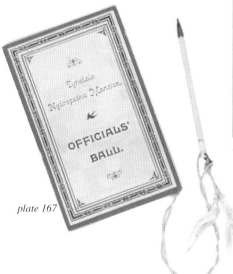

*plate 167*

*Above*
The left hand page of this 1894 dance card listed various dances, such as Circassian Circle, Waltz, Lancers, Quadrilles, etc. The opposite page had space for the names of proposed dancing partners.

WINTER GARDENS, HEXHAM HYDROPATHIC.

The Winter Gardens, which were added in 1907, are seen here with their original furnishings.

*plate 169*

**HEXHAM FLOWER SHOW AND BRASS BAND CONTEST**

THE THIRTY-FIFTH ANNUAL SHOW will be Held at the SPITAL PARK (by kind permission) On Wednesday, September 2nd 1874 Admission from Eleven in the morning to Two P.M. Two shillings; after Two, One shilling A GRAND BRASS BAND CONTEST will be Held, where £34 9s will be competed for.

☛ Entrance to the Show at Quatre Bras.

*Hexham Courant*          29th August 1874

# The Spital

The Spital, seen here c.1900, was so called because it was built near the site of St. Giles Hospital for husbandmen, born within Hexhamshire, who were lepers. In 1802 James Gibson (who later added Kirsopp to his name) bought the estate, demolished the old house and built this one. In 1951 Hexham Golf Club bought Spital House and Spital Parks, which extended to 128 acres.

*plate 170*

# *Hirings & Fairs*

The Market place was crowded at Martinmas, 11th November 1878, as it was the day of the Hirings. *plate 171*

Throughout the 19thc there were two hirings a year for single servants, one at May Day, the other at Martinmas. They ceased with the advent of World War II in 1939. People hoping to be hired, sometimes for only 6 months, would wear a token to denote their trade. Thatchers wore a token of straw and carters a piece of whipcord around their hats, whilst shepherds carried crooks.

*plate 172*

Each farm worker had to make an individual bargain with his employer, so wages fluctuated. Farmers did not always get the best of the bargain, as labourers often found it easy to move on to a more favourable situation.

**WANTED**, a HIND, at May-day next. None Need apply unless finding a bondager.
Apply to Mr J. Newton, Chollerton
*Hexham Courant*                23rd April 1870

A bondager was the term used for some female agricultural workers. They could be a female relative or an older single woman or widow, who would share the labourer's home and be available to work when required.

The hiring fairs brought in not only potential employers and employees but also were regarded as local holidays. Many visitors were attracted by amusements and side-shows which often included wax-works, shooting galleries, gambling games and donkey rides. The Temperance Association took action against the problems of drunkenness by offering alternative refreshments and entertainments. The Abbey was opened to visitors, offering organ recitals throughout the afternoon.

*plate 173*

A scene of activity on Hiring Day in the Market Place, c.1890.

plate 174

At an agricultural show, c.1890, Mr Brotherton holds the horse's head whilst Ralph Dodd leans on the rolley of Henry Bell &Sons. Turnouts like this were an important advertising and public-relations exercise at these events.

*plate 175*

A fair being held, c.1890, on the field at the top of Beaumont Street where William Cook had started his Fat Stock Auction Mart in 1870. The Abbey Hotel was built on this site in 1901 (see page 59).

## *Celebrations*

plate 176

Crowds gathering in the Market Place for the proclamation of King George V in 1910.

*plate 177*

Residents of Garden Terrace celebrate the end of World War 1 with a street party, 1918.

# *Domestic &*
# *Social Life*

*Left*
Children outside the Gem Picture Palace in the Market Place c.1900. Were they celebrating a special occasion? Although some have bare feet, many are dressed in good clothes.

*plate 178*

*Right*
A Pierrot Show on the Sele c.1905.

*plate 179*

*plate 180*

Competitors and officials pose in front of the pavilion at Prior's Flat in May 1896 during the Hexham Tennis Tournament. Tynedale Lawn Tennis Club was formed the following year.

*plate 181*

Mrs Sarah Harriet Forster (nee Featherstonehaugh) and her elder sister Janey photographed in the 1890s. They were living at Dodd's Yard, Market Street, during this time.

*plate 182*

Mrs Martha Cockfield (nee Smith) standing in front of the Spital c.1890, where she was employed as a seamstress. Martha and her gardener husband lived in Gilesgate.

Louisa A.Revitt standing outside 22
Alexandra Terrace, c.1900, when she
was aged about forty, and widowed.
Seated is her mother-in-law, Susan,
who was in her eighties when this
photograph was taken.

*plate 183*

*Right*
Mrs Hannah Turnbull and her daughter Annie, a dressmaker, in the doorway of 10 Dean Street, with a friend, c.1905.

*Below*
William Dunwoodie with his wife Ann and daughter Isabella outside their home at Cockshaw House c.1880. William Dunwoodie was an important hatter and glover and built Dunwoodie Terrace in the 1880s.

*plate 184*

*plate 185*

*plate 186*

An engraving by Edward Swinburne, c.1825, which shows Hexham from the north east, near Tyne Mills.

plate 187

This view c.1900, shows Hexham in the Tyne Valley from the south east.

*fig. 17*

Hexham town centre 1860.

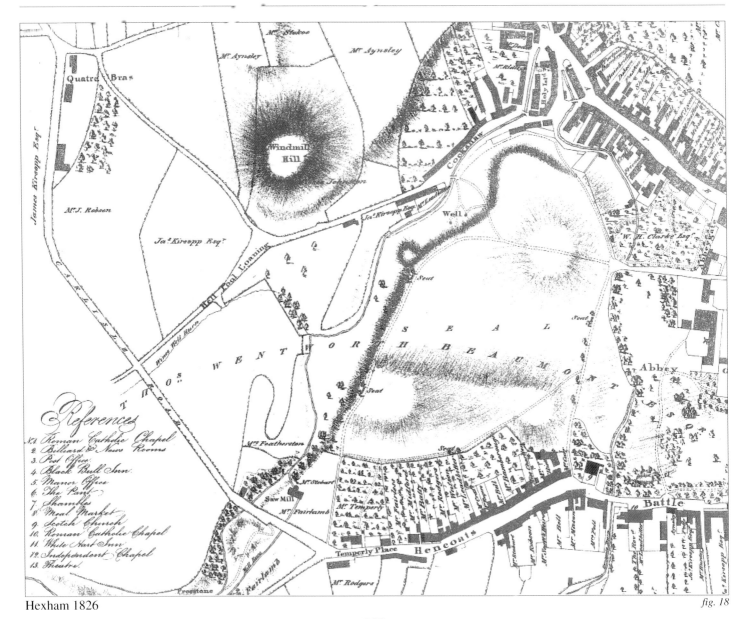

Hexham 1826

*fig. 18*

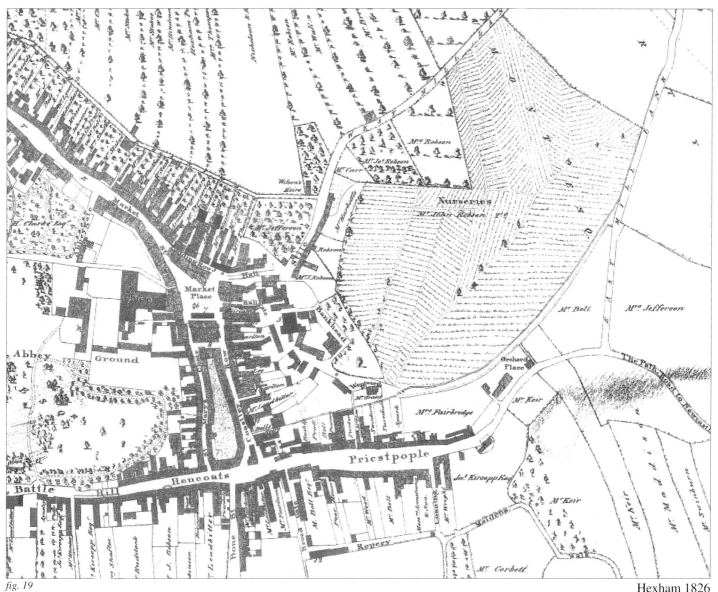

*fig. 19*

Hexham 1826

## In Hexham Abbey

Like spirits resurrected from the tomb
We stept from the dark slype's low vaulted gloom
Into the transept's soaring radiancy
Where from the lancets of the clerestory
Noon-sunshine streaming charged the pale sandstone
Of wall and pillar with a golden tone
Rich as the colour of the rock, fresh-hewn
From sheer Northumbrian hillsides to the tune
Of clinking hammer and chisel, in the days
When the aspiring spirit in life's praise
Soared in exultant fabrics of delight –
Earth quarried stuff exalted to the height
Of man's imagination, heaven-entranced.

And, as with eager footsteps we advanced
Through the South Transept with enraptured eyes,
From off our hearts fell the perplexities
Of these calamitious times ; and we forgot
Awhile the warring of nations and the lot
Of the battalioned youngsters doomed to march
Into annihilation – pier and arch
Springing in sunshine seeming still inspired
With the adoring ecstasy that fired
Those early craftsmen : and we recalled how man,
Builder and breaker since the world began
Betrayed by frailties of the mortal flesh,
Is yet a phoenix soul that springs afresh
Resilient to the imperishable gleam
Out of the self-wrought havoc of his dream,
From devastation fashioning anew
His vision ; and that to his best self true
Man, the destroyer, is Man the builder, too.

## John Pattison Gibson

Dead as the Romans he adored,
My father lies –
Yet can I see the light in his keen eyes
Leap, as the glitter of an unsheathed sword,
When, to the clarion of their names, awaoke
His proud and eager spirit ; ad he spoke
Of Hadrian's Wall, that strides from hill to hill
Along the wave-crest of the Great Whin Sill.

And surely now his spirit stands,
This crystal day,
When the first curlew calls, and bent and brae
Awaken to the Spring, above the lands
Of his hearts love, on Whinshiels' windt height,
With eyes that see the rampart, aquared and white,
New-builded, as when Hadrian first surveyed
Rome's arrogance against the North arrayed !

# Bessie Stokoe

He stood with the other young herds
At the Hiring to-day :
And I laughed and I chaffed and changed words
With every young hind of them all
As I stopped by the lollipop stall,
But never a word did he say.

He had straggly long straw-coloured hair
And a beard like a goat –
In his breeches a badly-stitched tear
That I longed, standing there in the crush,
To re-mend, as I hankered to brush
The ruddle and fluff from his coat.

But his bonnie blue eyes staring wide
Looked far beyond me,
As though on some distant fellside
His dogs were collecting the sheep,
And he anxiously watched them to keep
A young dog from running too free –

And I almost expected to hear
From the lips of the lad
A shrill whistle sing in my ear
As he eyed that green hillside to check
The fussy black frolicking speck
That was chasing the grey specks like mad.

So I left them, and went on my way
With a lad with black hair ;
And we swung and rode round all the day
To the racket of corncrake and gong :
But I never forget in the throng
The eyes with the faraway stare.

The jimmy-smart groom at my side
Had twinkling black eyes ;
But the grin on his mouth was too wide,
And his hands with my hands were too free :
So I took care to slip him at tea
As he turned round to pay for the pies.

And I left him alone on the seat
With the teapot and cups
And the two pies he's paid for to eat.
If he happens to think of the cause,
It may teach him to keep his red paws
For the handling of horses and pups.

But alone in the rain and the dark
As I made for the farm
I halted a moment to hark
To the sound of a shepherd's long stride :
And the shy lad stepped up to my side,
And I felt his arm link through my arm.

So it seems after all I'm to mend
Those breeches, and keep
That shaggy head clipped to the end,
And the shaggy chin clean, and to give
That coat a good brush – and to live
All my days in the odour of sheep.

*Silver token, approx 5cm diameter, engraved with the words*
*"George & Dragon Inn, Back St., Hexham, the property of Mrs H. Whyte".*
*Hannah Whyte was the landlady during the mid 19th century.*
*This token could possibly have been used to decorate a tobacco box used in the*
*inn or as a token given to coaching companies who called at the inn.*

Many thanks to Marjorie Dallison for her knowledge and advice, to Tom Kristensen for the design and layout of this book and to Liz Sobell for proof reading. Also to Northumberland Record Office staff, in particular Carol Scott and Keith Gilroy, and to Julian Harrop and Carolyn Ware of Beamish Museum; and to Neel Lever, Roger Guthrie, Philip Brooks, Elizabeth Bramwell, Edward Robson, Brian Bennison and Conrad Dickinson.

We would like to thank the following organizations and individuals who have kindly allowed us to reproduce their photographs, paintings and etchings in this book:

BEAMISH MUSEUM Regional Resource Centre - The following plates are reproduced by permission of Beamish Museum: plate 43 (5997), 50 (87867) 57 (24547), 75 (89873), 76 (59987), 78 (55950), 81 (89856), 84 (73685), 98 (93176), 108 (44593), 116 (84178), 117 (76865), 120 (5998/N), 122 (13685), 123 (28570), 126 (89867), 128 (10160), 136 (18689), 137 (18690), 147 (34920), 169 (163659), 174 (13139),176 (62958), 181 (12267), 185 (74526).
© Beamish Museum

BOOTS Archives Dept. - plate 51, by permission of Boots ©

BRITISH LIBRARY - The following plates are reproduced by permission of The British Library; plate 20 (K.Top vol XXXII f.48b) artist unknown, 17 (15543,f.16), 19 (15543,f.39), 24 (15543,f.38), 29 (15543,f.38), 95 (15543,f.45), 102 (15543,f.43), these last six are by Samuel Hieronymus Grimm. © The British Museum.

ENGLISH HERITAGE - The following plates are reproduced by permission of English Heritage, NMR: plate 37 (AA97/06025), 87 (BB92/20094), 104 (BB98/06023), 105 (AA97/05876), 133 (AA97/05217),141 (AA97/06021), 183 (BB98/06022), these photographs are by Alfred Newton & Sons. © N.M.R., English Heritage.

HEXHAM COURANT - for access to early copies for reference.

NEWCASTLE CITY LIBRARY, Local Studies Section - plate 45 © Newcastle City Library

NORTHUMBERLAND ARCHIVES SERVICE, Northumberland Record Office - The following plates are reproduced by permission of Northumberland Records Office: plate 33 (1896/1), 38 (ZLK plans), 107 (9595 FS), 171 (1876-C6-197), 186 (4733-28).
The following photographs are from the John Pattison Gibson Collection (© The Gibson Family) plate 10 (NRO 1876-F-2774), 14 (NRO 1876-F-2790), 34 (NRO 1876-F-0304), 44 (NRO 1876-F-3951), 83 (NRO 1876-F-2779), 84 (NRO 1876-F-2776), 85 (NRO 1876-F-4157),111 (NRO 1876-C6-188), 126 (NRO 1876-F-1323), 146 (NRO 1876-F-0303), 152 (NRO 1876-C6-205), 160 (NRO 1876-C6-135).
The following plates are photographs from Morton Charlton's book on *"Old Hexham"* : plate 127 (NRO 5845-2-132), 154 (NRO 5845-1-89), 155 (NRO 5845-2-070), 156 (NRO 5845-1-88), 161 (NRO 5845-2-060).
© Northumberland Record Office.

TYNE & WEAR MUSEUMS - The following paintings are reproduced by permission of Tyne & Wear Museums:
plate 1 - "Hexham Market Place" by William Bell Scott, Laing Art Gallery,
plate 2 - "The Smithy, Hexham Bridge End" by Ralph Hedley, Sunderland Museum & Art Gallery.
© Tyne & Wear Museums.

Conrad Dickinson: plates 8, 26, 49, 66, 71, 73, 134 & 135.
Arthur Iveson collection: plates 124, 125a, 125b & 175.
Edward Robson: plate 165.  Hexham Tennis Club: plate 180.
The Green Room Restaurant: plate 114.

Thanks are also due to those people who have kindly donated photographs to Colin Dallison's collection; apologies for not listing everyone by name.

**Figure Numbers**

Fig. 1: page 111 of the *History of Hexham* by A.B.Wright.
Fig. 2: Alms house report - NRO 1787 QSR, Northumberland
      Record Office.
Fig. 3: Pigot's Directory 1822.
Figs. 4, 5, 6, 13, 14 & 17:1860 map - OS 94.6  25 inch
Fig. 7: plan of House of Correction 1849 - NRO 691,
      Northumberland Record Office
Fig. 8: page 25 of the *History of Hexham* by A.B.Wright.
Figs. 9 & 10: Newcastle Railway 1835-1985 by P.R.B.Brooks.
Fig. 11: 1825 pamphlet, author's collection.
Fig. 12: Railway timetable 1845, Northumberland Record
      Office.
Fig. 15: Phipps bill-head, Arthur Iveson collection.
Fig. 16: page 42 of *Homecoming* by W.W.Gibson
Figs. 18 & 19: Woods map 1826.
Poems on 154 & 155 - *Homecoming* by W. W. Gibson

The Hexham War Memorial Cross.